CHRISTIANITY
E✝PLORED

ENGLISH MADE EASY EDITION

Authentic

10 09 08 07 06 05 04   7 6 5 4 3 2 1

First published in 2004 by Authentic Media
9 Holdom Avenue, Bletchley, Milton Keynes, MK1 1QR, UK
and PO Box 1047, Waynesboro, GA 30830-2047, USA
www.authenticmedia.co.uk

BRITISH LIBRARY CATALOGUING IN PUBLICATION DATA
A catalogue record for this book is available from the British Library

ISBN 1-85078-576-7

Designed by Diane Bainbridge
Illustrations by Alex Webb-Peploe
Print Management by Adare Carwin

CHRISTIANITY EXPLORED

ENGLISH MADE EASY EDITION

STUDY GUIDE

Before We Begin

Over the next eight weeks we will explore Christianity by seeing what the Bible has to say about Jesus Christ.

In particular, we will explore three questions about Jesus:

- who was he?

- why did he come?

- what does it mean to follow him?

The Bible contains 66 books. Many human authors wrote these books over 1500 years. God's Holy Spirit inspired each author. When we read the Bible, we are reading God's words – exactly what he wants us to know.

The Bible is divided into two main sections: the Old Testament and the New Testament. The Old Testament was written before Jesus was born and the New Testament was written after Jesus was born.

In this course we will read the book of Mark (also known as Mark's Gospel), which is a historical account of Jesus' life.

Mark's Gospel is divided up into chapters and each chapter is divided into individual verses, all of which are numbered. So 'Mark 1:1 – 3:6' refers to the book of Mark, chapter 1, verse 1, through to chapter 3, verse 6. All the Bible references in this *Study Guide* are written in this way.

During the course we will study various passages from Mark's Gospel. You may also ask any questions about Christianity.

So who was Jesus? Why did he come? And what does it mean to follow him?

What is Christianity?

Welcome to *Christianity Explored*.

What is your name? Why did you decide to come on the course?

If you could ask God one question, and you knew it would be answered, what would it be?

What do people usually think Christianity is about?

☐ Christianity is about being a good person

☐ Christianity is about going to church

☐ Christianity is a Western religion

☐ Christianity is about following the teachings of Jesus Christ

☐ Christianity is _____

Read Mark 1:1 aloud.

1   **What do we learn about Christianity from this verse? (Note that the word 'gospel' means 'good news'.)**

_____

_____

_____

_____

_____

_____

2   **Some people criticise Christianity. They say:**

'It is a list of rules.'
'It is about going to church and pretending to be a good person.'
'It is boring.'

How does Mark answer these criticisms in Mark 1:1?

_____

_____

_____

_____

_____

?! Do you have any comments or questions?

Each week you will explore a few chapters of Mark on your own at home. You will read the whole Gospel of Mark before the end of the course.

Before next week read Mark 1:1 – 3:6. Write down any questions you have and ask them next time.

Jesus – Who Was He?

 Christianity is good news about Jesus Christ...

Who do people today think Jesus was?

☐ A good teacher

☐ A prophet

☐ A political leader

☐ God

☐ Other _____

 Read Mark 2:1–12 aloud.

1   Are there any words you do not understand?

2   What problem did the four men have? (see verses 2–4)

3   How did the men solve this problem? (see verse 4)

4 What did the men expect Jesus to do for the paralytic?

_____

_____

_____

_____

5 What did Jesus do? (see verse 5) Why do you think he did that?

_____

_____

_____

_____

6 Why were the religious teachers so angry? (see verses 6–7)

_____

_____

_____

_____

7 What is the answer to Jesus' question in verse 9?

_____

_____

_____

8   Why did Jesus heal the man? (see verses 10–12)

_____

_____

_____

_____

9   In Mark 2:10 Jesus calls himself the 'Son of Man'. The prophet Daniel described the son of man 500 years before Mark:

'In my vision at night I looked, and there before me was one like a son of man, coming with the clouds of heaven... He was given authority, glory and sovereign power; all peoples, nations and men of every language worshipped him.' (Daniel 7:13–14)

In your own words, how did Daniel describe the son of man?

_____

_____

_____

_____

10 What did Jesus expect people to understand when he called himself the 'Son of Man' in Mark 2:10?

_____

_____

_____

11 What does this event in Mark tell us about who Jesus is?

_____

_____

_____

12 Who do you think Jesus is?

_____

_____

_____

Jesus has power and authority to forgive sin.

Mark also shows that Jesus has power and authority:

- to teach (see for example Mark 1:21–22)

- over evil spirits (see for example Mark 1:23–27)

- over sickness (see for example Mark 1:29–34)

- over nature (see for example Mark 4:35–41)

- and even over death (see for example Mark 5:35–42)

The evidence in Mark's Gospel suggests that Jesus was a man with the power and authority of God himself. He is, as Mark says in Mark 1:1, the Son of God.

?! Do you have any comments or questions?

_____

_____

_____

_____

_____

Before next week read Mark 3:7 – 5:43. Write down any questions you have and ask them next time.

_____

_____

_____

_____

_____

_____

_____

_____

_____

_____

_____

Jesus – Why Did He Come?

 Christianity is good news about Jesus Christ, the Son of God...

What do you think is the world's greatest problem?

- ☐ War
- ☐ Poverty
- ☐ Pollution
- ☐ Racism
- ☐ Greed
- ☐ Other _____

In last week's study, what was the paralytic's greatest problem?

Read Mark 12:28–30 aloud.

1 Are there any words you do not understand?

2 How should we treat God?

3 How do we treat God?

None of us have loved God as we should. Instead of loving God, we have all turned away from him. We have all rebelled against God. This is called sin.

Read Mark 7:20–23 aloud.

4   Are there any words you do not understand?

_____

_____

_____

_____

_____

5   Where is our sin?

_____

_____

_____

6   What is the result of our sin?

_____

_____

_____

The evils that come out of our hearts make us 'unclean' before God. God cannot ignore our sin because of his purity and justice. That is our greatest problem.

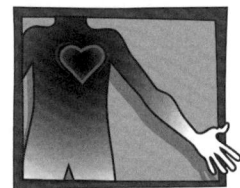

Read Mark 9:43–48 aloud.

7   Are there any words you do not understand?

_____

_____

_____

_____

_____

_____

8   How will God judge our sin?

_____

_____

_____

_____

9   Why is Jesus' warning so severe? (see verses 43 and 48)

_____

_____

_____

_____

_____

10 **What would you say if someone said to you, 'When I die God will be pleased with me because I am a good person'?**

_____

_____

_____

_____

_____

We have all rebelled against God.
We all face his judgement.
We all need to be rescued.

That is why Jesus came.

Jesus said, 'It is not the healthy who need a doctor, but the sick. I have not come to call the righteous, but sinners' (Mark 2:17).

Jesus came to rescue us from the judgement our sin deserves. Next week we will learn how he does that.

?! Do you have any comments or questions?

_____

_____

_____

_____

_____

Before next week read Mark 6:1 – 7:37. Write down any questions you have and ask them next time.

_____

_____

_____

_____

_____

_____

_____

_____

_____

_____

_____

Jesus – His Death

 Christianity is good news about Jesus Christ, the Son of God. Jesus came to rescue us from sin, judgement and hell...

Where do you see crosses today?

_____

_____

_____

_____

In Jesus' day, men were punished by being nailed to a wooden cross and left to die. It was a terrible and shameful thing to die in this way. God spoke about this kind of punishment hundreds of years before when he said, '...anyone who is hung on a tree is under God's curse' (Deuteronomy 21:23).

Jesus predicts his own death three times. Read aloud:

Mark 8:31   Mark 9:30–31   Mark 10:32–34

What does Jesus say 'must' and 'will' happen? (Remember that 'Son of Man' is Jesus' way of referring to himself.)

 Read Mark 15:33–39 aloud.

1   Are there any words you do not understand?

Read Mark 15:33 aloud again.

2   What unusual event occurred at mid-day (the sixth hour) as Jesus was dying?

_____

_____

_____

_____

3   In the Bible, darkness is a sign of God's anger and judgement. What is surprising about the focus of God's anger?

_____

_____

_____

_____

_____

God's judgement fell on Jesus, instead of us.

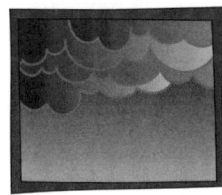

Read Mark 15:34 aloud again.

4   What was the relationship between Jesus and his Father before the cross? (see Mark 1:9–11 and Mark 9:7)

_____

_____

_____

_____

_____

5   What happened between Jesus and his Father at the cross?

_____

_____

_____

_____

_____

Jesus was abandoned so that we do not have to be.

Read Mark 15:37–38 aloud again.

6 **What happened in the temple in Jerusalem when Jesus died?**

_____

_____

_____

7 **The curtain in the middle of the temple prevented sinful people from entering God's presence in the Most Holy Place. It also protected the people from God's holiness. Only once a year, a priest was able to go through the curtain and enter God's presence in the Most Holy Place. But the priest could only enter after he made special sacrifices. How did Jesus' death change our relationship with God?**

_____

_____

_____

_____

We can be accepted because Jesus died for us. The way to God is now open.

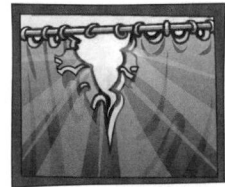

8   Isaiah prophesied about Jesus' death 700 years earlier:

'He suffered the things we should have suffered. He took on himself the pain that should have been ours... But the servant was pierced because we had sinned. He was crushed because we had done what was evil... All of us are like sheep. We have wandered away from God. All of us have turned to our own way. And the Lord has placed on his servant the sins of all of us.' (Isaiah 53:4–6, NIrV)

Why did God's judgement fall on his servant Jesus?

_____

_____

_____

_____

_____

_____

9   **Will you let Jesus pay for your sin?**

_____

_____

_____

_____

_____

_____

At the cross Jesus took on himself our sin and God's punishment for our sin.

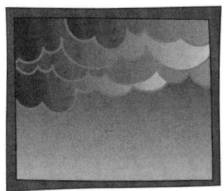

Jesus paid the price for our sin so that we never have to.

As Jesus died, the curtain in the temple was torn in two from top to bottom. This illustrates the fact that Jesus' death opens the way for sinful people to come into God's presence.

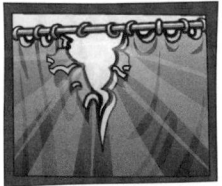

Jesus' death rescues us from God's judgement.

?! Do you have any comments or questions?

_____

_____

_____

_____

_____

Before next week read Mark 8:1 – 9:32. Write down any questions you have and ask them next time.

_____

_____

_____

_____

_____

_____

_____

_____

_____

_____

_____

_____

What is Grace?

 Christianity is good news about Jesus Christ, the Son of God. Jesus came to rescue us from sin, judgement and hell by dying on a cross. He took the punishment we deserve...

If you died today, why should God let you into heaven?

God should let me into heaven because _____

_____

_____

_____

_____

Read Mark 10:17–22 aloud.

---

1   Are there any words you do not understand?

2   What did the rich man want to know? (see verse 17)

3   What commandments did the man say he had kept? (see verses 19–20)

4 Read Mark 12:28–31. What did Jesus say was the most important commandment?

_____

_____

_____

_____

5 How did Jesus show the rich man that he had not loved God as he should? (see Mark 10:21–22)

_____

_____

_____

_____

6 The rich man loved his wealth more than he loved God. What other things do people love more than God?

_____

_____

_____

_____

None of us deserve to enter heaven because none of us have loved God as we should.

Read Mark 10:13–16 aloud.

7   Are there any words you do not understand?

_____

_____

_____

_____

_____

_____

_____

_____

8   What did the children need to do in order to belong to the kingdom of God? (see verse 14)

_____

_____

9   How can anyone enter the kingdom of God? (see verse 15)

_____

_____

_____

10 What was wrong with the man's question in verse 17?

_____

_____

_____

11 Ephesians 2:8 says, 'It is by grace you have been saved, through faith – and this not from yourselves, it is the gift of God – not by works, so that no-one can boast.' In your own words, what saves you?

_____

_____

_____

We are all like the man in Mark 10. We do not love God with all our heart.

We deserve to be punished.

But God the Father loves us so much that he sent his Son to rescue us. He suffered the terrible judgement that our sins deserve.

We cannot earn God's forgiveness and eternal life by doing good things. God gives us the gift of forgiveness and eternal life if we simply put our trust in Jesus Christ. And that is grace: God behaving towards us in a way we do not deserve.

?! Do you have any comments or questions?

_____

_____

_____

_____

_____

Before next week read Mark 9:33 – 11:25. Write down any questions you have and ask them next time.

_____

_____

_____

_____

_____

_____

_____

_____

_____

_____

_____

_____

Jesus – His Resurrection

 Christianity is good news about Jesus Christ, the Son of God. Jesus came to rescue us from sin, judgement and hell by dying on a cross. He took the punishment we deserve. It is only by God's grace that we can be saved...

What do you think happens to us after we die?

Week 6

Read Mark 15:42–16:8 aloud.

1 **Are there any words you do not understand?**

2 **Why did the women go to Jesus' tomb? (see Mark 16:1)**

3 **What were they thinking about as they went to the tomb? (verses 2–3)**

4 What did they find when they got to the tomb? (verses 4–6)

_____

_____

_____

_____

5 The empty tomb should not have surprised the women. Why not? (see verse 7 and Mark 14:28)

_____

_____

_____

_____

6 According to the following verses, what did Jesus say he came to do?

Mark 8:31 _____

_____

_____

Mark 9:30–31 _____

_____

_____

Mark 10:32–34 _____

_____

7   Why did Jesus have to do these things? (see Mark 10:45)

_____

_____

_____

_____

8   We have seen Jesus' power and authority over many things. What does his resurrection tell us about him?

_____

_____

_____

_____

9   How did the women react to Jesus' resurrection? (see Mark 16:8)

_____

_____

_____

_____

10   What does this tell us about their understanding of Jesus and what he came to do?

_____

_____

_____

11 Jesus said, 'I am the resurrection and the life. He who believes in me will live, even though he dies; and whoever lives and believes in me will never die' (John 11:25–26). What does Jesus' resurrection mean for us if we trust him?

_____

_____

_____

_____

God must punish our sin.

The punishment for sin is death and hell.

When Jesus died on the cross and rose from the dead, he took God's punishment for our sin and overcame death.

His resurrection offers great hope. It proves that there will be eternal life for those who trust in what Jesus did at the cross.

However, the resurrection is also a warning. If we do not let Jesus pay for our sin, we will pay for it ourselves for ever in hell (Mark 9:47–48) when Jesus returns to earth to judge us (Mark 8:38).

?! Do you have any comments or questions?

Before next week read Mark 11:27 – 13:37. Write down any questions you have and ask them next time.

What is a Christian?

Christianity is good news about Jesus Christ, the Son of God. Jesus came to rescue us from sin, judgement and hell by dying on a cross. He took the punishment we deserve. It is only by God's grace that we can be saved. Jesus rose from the dead, so we know that those who trust in him will have eternal life...

What do you think when you hear the word 'Christian'?

_____

_____

_____

_____

Read Mark 8:27–38 aloud.

1   Are there any words you do not understand?

   **Who is Jesus?**

 Read Mark 8:27–29 aloud again.

2   What did Jesus ask his disciples in verse 27?

3 According to verse 28, who did most people say Jesus was?

_____

_____

_____

_____

4 Peter answered Jesus' question correctly. According to Mark 8:29 and Mark 1:1, who is Jesus?

_____

_____

_____

_____

5 How would you answer Jesus' question in verse 29?

_____

_____

_____

_____

_____

_____

What did Jesus come to do?

 Read Mark 8:31–33 aloud again.

6   'Christ' is a title. It means, 'the Anointed One'.
    Anointing showed that God had chosen someone for
    a special purpose. 'Christ' describes Jesus' position
    and authority as the King who came to bring people
    into his kingdom.

    The people of Israel were expecting the Christ to
    come and save them from their enemies. What did
    Jesus say he had come to do? (see verse 31)

    _____

    _____

    _____

7   According to verse 32, how did Peter react to Jesus'
    teaching?

    _____

    _____

    _____

    _____

8 Why did Peter react like this? (see verse 33)

_____

_____

_____

9 God the Father's plan for his Son, Jesus Christ, was very different from Peter's idea. Think about what you have learned already. Why did Jesus have to be killed and rise again?

_____

_____

What does it mean to follow Jesus?

  Read Mark 8:34–38 aloud again.

10 What does Jesus demand of those who want to follow him? (see verse 34)

_____

_____

_____

11 Why is it wise to follow Jesus, according to verses 35–38?

_____

_____

_____

_____

12 In what ways would you have to deny yourself to follow Jesus?

_____

_____

_____

_____

13 From what you have learned in Mark 8, describe what a Christian is. Use your own words.

_____

_____

_____

_____

14 Would you use the words above to describe yourself?

_____

_____

_____

_____

Who is Jesus?

Jesus is the Christ, the Son of God.

What did Jesus come to do?

Jesus came to die as a ransom for many. The only way sinful people can come back into a relationship with God is by Jesus dying in their place.

What does it mean to follow Jesus?

Jesus says, 'If anyone would come after me, he must deny himself and take up his cross and follow me.' Denying self means no longer living for ourselves but for Jesus. Taking up our cross means being prepared to follow him, whatever the cost.

A Christian is a person who trusts and obeys Jesus.

?! Do you have any comments or questions?

_____

_____

_____

_____

_____

Before next week read Mark 14:1 – 16:8. Write down any questions you have and ask them next time.

_____

_____

_____

_____

_____

_____

_____

_____

_____

_____

_____

What Next?

 Christianity is good news about Jesus Christ, the Son of God. Jesus came to rescue us from sin, judgement and hell by dying on a cross. He took the punishment we deserve. It is only by God's grace that we can be saved. Jesus rose from the dead, so we know that those who trust in him will have eternal life. A Christian is a person who trusts and obeys Jesus.

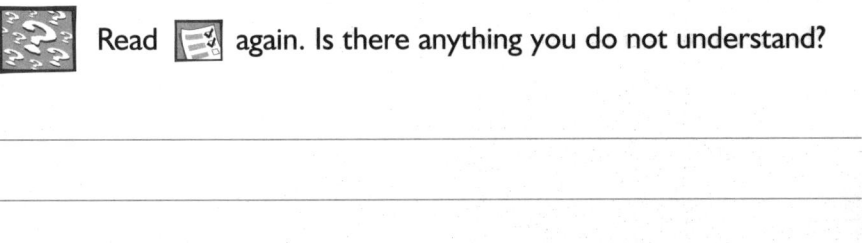 Read again. Is there anything you do not understand?

_____

_____

_____

_____

Read Mark 4:1–20 aloud.

1   Jesus often taught people by telling parables. A
     parable is a story with a spiritual lesson. In verses 3–8
     Jesus tells the story. In verses 13–20 he explains the
     lesson. Are there any words you do not understand?

_____

_____

_____

_____

_____

_____

_____

_____

_____

2   What does the 'seed' represent? (compare verse 3
     with verse 14)

_____

_____

_____

_____

3   What happens when people hear God's word in verse 15?

_____

_____

_____

_____

_____

4   What happens when people hear God's word in verses 16–17?

_____

_____

_____

_____

5   What does it mean that a person who hears God's word 'has no root'? (verse 17)

_____

_____

_____

_____

6 **What happens when people hear God's word in verses 18–19?**

_____

_____

_____

_____

_____

7 **How do worries, money and other desires choke God's word?**

_____

_____

_____

_____

8 **What happens when people hear God's word in verse 20?**

_____

_____

_____

9 Which of these responses do you most relate to?

?! Do you have any comments or questions?

Jesus is clear about the right way to respond to God's word. 'The time has come,' he said. 'The kingdom of God is near. Repent and believe the good news!' (Mark 1:15).

That means we must turn from what we know is wrong and trust in what Jesus has done for us on the cross.

You may still have questions. Or it may be that you understand who Jesus is, why he came, and what it means to follow him. You believe that Jesus is who he claims to be. You know you have rebelled against God and need him to rescue you. You want to accept God's forgiveness.

Here is a prayer that you can pray if you are ready to repent and believe.

Lord God, I have not loved you with all my heart, soul, mind and strength. I am sorry for the way I have lived. I have rebelled against you in so many ways. I now understand who Jesus is. I understand that when he died on the cross, he was taking the punishment in my place. He did this so that I could be forgiven and have eternal life. I gratefully accept that gracious gift. From now on, please give me the desire to obey you. Help me to live the Christian life, whatever the cost.

Further Exploration

IF YOU ARE NOT A CHRISTIAN

Thank you for coming. Many people come to the course two or three times in order to help them understand Christianity. You may want to take the course again. Or you might want to meet with a Christian if you have other questions that you were unable to ask before.

IF YOU HAVE BECOME A CHRISTIAN

You are about to explore an amazing new life! Jesus promises that anyone who sincerely asks can be sure that their sins have been forgiven. It does not matter what you feel like. If you have put your trust in Jesus and are living to please him, you are now one of God's children.

When you become a Christian, God comes to live in you by his Holy Spirit (John 14:16–17). He is always with you. He will help you, guide you, comfort you, show you your sin and change you, enabling you to follow Jesus.

The next two pages will help you as you begin the Christian life:

As you begin the Christian life, we want to encourage you to do the following:

Read the Bible

God speaks to us through the Bible (2 Timothy 3:16–17). If you want to develop and maintain a relationship with God, you must make time to read the Bible each day.

Pray

When we read the Bible, God speaks to us. When we pray, we speak to God. You do not need to use special words. Prayer is simply speaking to God (Philippians 4:6–7). Although you can pray at any time, it is good to set aside a regular time each day.

Meet with other Christians

It is not easy being a Christian, so it is vital to meet with others who will encourage you (Hebrews 10:24–25). The best way to do this is to go to church. It is very important to find a church that teaches God's word faithfully, where the people support you, and where you are able to serve others. (Visit www.ifesworld.org if you want to meet with Christian students in your own country.)

There may be times when you doubt that you are really a Christian. You may wonder if God has really forgiven all your sins and loves you. You may ask yourself if being a Christian is really worth it. When you feel like that, remind yourself of:

Jesus' promise

Jesus said that he came to earth not to call good people, but to call sinners (Mark 2:17).

Jesus' death

When Jesus died, the temple curtain was torn from top to bottom. This shows that Jesus' death provides the way for us to have a relationship with God (Mark 15:38). Remember that you are saved not because of something you do. You are saved because of what Jesus has already done.

Jesus' resurrection

The result of sin is death. When Jesus died he paid the penalty for our sin. Death was not the end for Jesus. He rose from the dead and – because you have put your trust in him – you will have eternal life (Mark 16:6). As long as you trust in Jesus, you are sure of a wonderful eternity in heaven with him.

Other **Christianity Explored** resources are available from
www.christianityexplored.com